COAST

COAST

WHERE THE LAND MEETS THE SEA

DAVID ROSS

amber
BOOKS

Published by
Amber Books Ltd
United House
North Road
London
N7 9DP
United Kingdom
www.amberbooks.co.uk
Instagram: amberbooksltd
Facebook: www.facebook.com/amberbooks
Twitter: @amberbooks

Project Editor: Kieron Connolly
Designer: Mark Batley
Picture Research: Terry Forshaw

ISBN: 978-1-78274-898-4

Printed in China

Contents

Introduction

The edge of the sea has always faced humanity with a challenge: an obstacle to movement, or an open road to new places and discoveries? A point of departure, or of arrival? Coastlines give hints of the Earth's history long before life emerged. Ever since the whole planet was mapped, people have noted the way in which certain land-masses seemed to match each other's shape, like jigsaw pieces, especially noticeable between Africa and South America. We know now that is not a coincidence: they once formed part of a giant continent which existed before the Atlantic Ocean was formed.

The Earth has a great deal of coastline – around 1,635,000km (1,021,875 miles), which is more than 40 times the extent of the Equator. The sea itself has an endless fascination. Its moods and behaviour reflect our own, from contemplative calm or sparkling liveliness to ominous swells and raging storms. We can measure and forecast its tides and trace its great currents, but some things are unpredictable. Cyclonic storms or deep seismic events create surges and tsunamis that can ravage a coastline and reach far inland. Perhaps the eternal attraction of coastal scenery lies partly in that sense of uncertainty: even the most placid sandy beach is a frontier between the security of dry land and the great unknown.

ABOVE:
Iveragh Peninsula, County Kerry, Ireland
The Ring of Kerry's beautiful Atlantic coast.
OPPOSITE:
Edava, Kerala, India
Stones have been placed on the cliff edge in an effort to protect the eroding coastline.

The Americas

Two continents, or one? Joined by a narrow isthmus, North and South America stretch from the Arctic to the sub-Antarctic, fronting two great oceans and, in the case of the north, holding great lakes that are seas in themselves. For some 30,000 years up to around 12,000 BCE, North America and Asia were joined by a land connection which enabled the first known human inhabitants of the Americas to come from the Asian side and migrate southwards. The Isthmus of Panama is much more ancient, around 2.8 million years old, though still recent in geological time. Its formation, as with many other significant landscape features across the globe, was due to the collision of the great tectonic plates which float and move in the Earth's lithosphere – the crust and upper mantle. There are many tectonic plates, but nine major ones. Their movement is slow: the vastest, the Pacific Plate, moves northwards at a rate of 7cm (2.75in) a year, but their force is enormous, building up mountain ranges, causing massive rifts, opening up chains of volcanic activity and moving entire continents.

Another consequence left by these slow convulsions over billions of years is found in the variety of rock types: sedimentary rocks formed of sand, mud and shells deposited on ocean floors; metamorphic rocks, which are sedimentary rocks forced deep into the crust and hardened by heat and pressure; and igneous rocks, the solidified outpourings of volcanic action.

Once the rock is exposed on the surface, other forces get to work: flowing water, wind and ice. To these may be added biological activity. Two species have had a major influence on coastal landforms. The older is the coral polyp, the newer is the human race.

OPPOSITE:
Lake Argentino, Argentina
Glacier-fringed, this 'Silver Lake' gets its name from the meltwater which flows into it. The largest freshwater lake in Argentina, it is set in the Los Glaciares National Park, which was declared a UNESCO World Heritage Site in 1981.

LEFT:

Cormorants, Patagonia, Argentina
Four species of cormorant, or shag, are native to the Patagonian coast, including the imperial shag, whose distinctive crests appear during the breeding season. These seabirds are gregarious, living in small groups, and making nests among the rocks out of seaweed and grass.

OPPOSITE:

Perito Moreno Glacier, Lake Argentino, Argentina
More than 30km (18.75 miles) long and 5km (3.1 miles) wide at its end, this is one of the most active glaciers in South America, with large fragments frequently calving from its cliff-like edge into Lake Argentino.

PREVIOUS PAGE:

'La Portada', Antofagasta, Chile

These 50m (164ft) high cliffs are formed of layered sandstone laid down in the Miocene and Pliocene eras, set on a base of dark Jurassic rocks, and topped by a thick covering of fossilized shells from an ancient sea-bed. With minimal rainfall, this is one of the driest areas on Earth.

OPPOSITE:

Bottlenose Dolphins, Peru

The Pacific waters off Peru's coast are home to large numbers of fish which in turn support a permanent population of numerous species of dolphins, including these bottlenose dolphins. Now sufficiently rare, the bottlenose dolphin has been declared a protected species.

RIGHT:

Cabo de la Vela, La Guajira, Colombia

On Colombia's Caribbean coast, this remote headland – the 'Cape of the Sail' – is a still undeveloped spot, popular with more adventurous travellers. The local Wayúu people have adapted their lifestyle to the desert conditions.

ABOVE:
Pacific Coast, Costa Rica
The jungle reaches right to the edge of the Pacific Ocean in Costa Rica, and even beyond it, with these trees battling to survive on a wave-eroded stump of rock in the salt-laden, windy tidal zone.

RIGHT:
Corumbau, Bahia, Brazil
This old fishing village on the Atlantic coast of Brazil's Bahia state is the centre of a 'marine extractive reserve' intended to conserve fish stocks for the local boatmen. Coral reefs offshore help to sustain a variety of marine life.

LEFT:
**Bartolomé Island,
Galápagos Islands, Ecuador**
A Galápagos Hawk, one
of the many unique species
for which this island group
is famous, hovers above
the volcanic cliffs of its
uninhabited islet. Their diet
is primarily locusts and giant
centipedes. These birds are
rated as vulnerable on the
IUCN Red List of
threatened species.

RIGHT:
**Pinnacle Rock, Bartolomé
Island, Galápagos Islands,
Ecuador**
Hardened lava from a
volcanic period some two
million years ago forms
a distinctive tilting spike.
Beneath it, Galápagos
penguins breed and human
visitors enjoy snorkelling.

OPPOSITE:

Punta del Diablo Beach, Uruguay

Fishing boats drawn up on the beach show the original activity of the village of Punta del Diablo. A tranquil place, the reason for its 'Devil's Point' name is not clear. Sand dunes stretch away on both sides of the rocky point.

RIGHT:

Cozumel Island, Yucatán, Mexico

Cozumel Island is a limestone outcrop off the Yucatán peninsula, in the Caribbean Sea. Its rugged surface shows typical pitting caused by water erosion. The old log, washed in from the sea and placed upright, might be considered a work of art.

Malibu, California, USA
The Malibu Coast is a
34-kilometre (21-mile)
strip of fine sandy beaches
and rocky points along the
Pacific fringe. Famed for its
Hollywood star residents
and its surfing, it is one of
California's most popular
resorts. The wooded hills
above have suffered in recent
years from wildfires.

Cabo San Lucas, Baja California Sur, Mexico

On the southern tip of the Baja California peninsula, where the Pacific Ocean and the Sea of Cortez meet, are the spectacular granite cliffs of 'Land's End'. Sea lions live in the water here. In October at low tide, it's possible to walk out under the arch.

Thor's Well, Oregon, USA

Just at the tidal edge, Thor's Well is a bowl-shaped hole, possibly a collapsed sea cave, open at the bottom so that the incoming tide surges up, spills over and drains back again, making it seem as if the sea is being sucked in. It's a treacherous place when the waves are high.

Florida, USA
Lightning flashes usually occur on the outer edges of tropical storms. Intensive bursts of lightning closer to the centre are considered by some scientists to herald an intensification of storm conditions, though evidence also suggests that they may signal a lessening of intensity. Much research is going on in this field.

Exuma Keys, Bahamas
Situated on the Tropic of Cancer, the 365 Caribbean islands of the Bahamas make a pattern of dark green vegetation against brilliant white sand and turquoise-blue water. Mostly small and uninhabited, they have provided the background to numerous films. Their chequered history includes piracy and slavery, in contrast to the present calm.

Driftwood Beach, Jekyll Island, Georgia, USA
Jekyll is the smallest of Georgia's barrier islands, looking out to the Atlantic. 'Driftwood' is a misnomer: these trees once grew tall here, and their almost sculptural remains, bleached by sunlight, are the result of soil erosion exposing the roots. The whole island is gradually shifting southwards.

LEFT:

Lake Michigan, USA
In periods of extreme cold, known as the 'polar vortex', the great lake partially freezes over. Warmer weather then has the effect of creating shards as the ice breaks up, making remarkable patterns of ice-plates and light.

ABOVE:

Lake Michigan, USA
Lake Michigan is famous for the variety of pebbles found along its shoreline, including rare Septarian brown stones, laced with white calcite, as well as more common water-smoothed sandstone, limestone, granites and basalt. Snow melt and soil movements regularly bring new specimens to the surface.

LEFT:

Indian River, Dagsboro, Delaware, USA
Largely filling a one-time valley now invaded by the sea, Indian River was named after a Native American Blackfoot tribe that settled here in the 17th century. Broadening into a wide bay, it is shut off from the open sea by a narrow strip of land which is now maintained as the Delaware Seashore State Park.

OPPOSITE:

Acadia National Park, Maine, USA
The varied rocks of this mountainous island are a guide to the movement of the Earth's tectonic plates and to geological history in general. Beginning as sands and mud on an ocean floor close to the Equator, they solidified, were plunged deep into the planet's crust, thrust up, carried northwards, buried under ice caps and exposed once again.

BELOW:

York Beach, Maine, USA
Situated on a flat sandy bar, with the ocean in front and creeks and ponds behind, these houses, often second homes or holiday cottages, are at risk from rising sea levels and storm surges. As in many other coastal communities, protection measures are under discussion.

RIGHT:

Portsmouth, New Hampshire, USA
A quiet part of the waterfront of this historic town, incorporated in 1653. In sailing ship days it was a busy shipbuilding and maritime trading centre, and much of its architectural heritage has been preserved, making it a popular destination for visitors.

LEFT:

Grand Island, New Hampshire, USA

A winter sunrise on a still morning silhouettes a leafless tree. Across the bay, Whaleback Lighthouse, erected by the US Army Corps of Engineers in 1872, marks the estuary of the Piscataqua River. Beyond is the open Atlantic Ocean.

RIGHT

Castle Hill Lighthouse, Newport, Rhode Island, USA

Niched into the craggy cliffs above Narragansett Bay, this small lighthouse was built with granite blocks in 1890 and still protects vessels bound for Portsmouth, New Hampshire, and Newport, Rhode Island. Once manned by a team of keepers, it has been automated since 1957.

LEFT:

Wildwood, New Jersey, USA
Miles of sandy beach stretch on each side, making Wildwood a popular resort for the surrounding urban areas. It stands on a barrier island, linked by bridge to the mainland.

ABOVE:

Manhattan, New York, USA
Seen from Brooklyn Bridge Park, Lower Manhattan glitters in the sunset. The old poles in the foreground, intended to stabilize mud-flow and maintain channels, will have to be replaced as the sea level gradually rises.

OVERLEAF:

Na Pali, Kauai, Hawaii, USA
The *na pali* are these massive cliffs, reaching up to 1,200m (3,940ft) in the Na Pali Coast State Park. The result of a huge undersea eruption some five million years ago, the entire island is a mound of volcanic rock, weathered and shaped by water and wind, with a variety of microclimatic zones in its deep canyons and valleys.

Kenai Peninsula, Alaska, USA
Between Cook Inlet and the Gulf of Alaska, this rugged, thickly wooded peninsula holds both a national park and a national wildlife refuge area. Fed by mountain glaciers and rain, salmon-rich rivers run to deep fjords that reach far inland. In the wilderness areas, much of the coastline is impenetrable and accessible only by boat.

Knight Inlet, British Columbia, Canada
Grizzly and black bears live in the forest zone lining this 125-kilometre (80-mile) inlet of the Pacific Ocean. The water here is also home to dolphins, sea lions and porpoises, as well as sometimes Minke whales and orcas. Its natural resources have sustained indigenous communities for around 6,000 years.

LEFT:

Baffin Island, Nunavut, Canada
Baffin Island, between the Nunavut mainland and Greenland, is the world's fifth-largest. Here a typical glacier tongue drops steeply to the sea, close to the settlement of Iqaluit. Discolouration of the ice is caused by dust and particulate matter carried in the atmosphere from other parts of the world.

OPPOSITE:

Frobisher Bay, Iqaluit, Nunavut, Canada
Iqaluit ('place of many fish') is the largest settlement and capital of Nunavut, and a vibrant centre of Inuit cultural life. In winter the temperature can fall to −29°C (−20°F), and the warmest month is July, with an average 7°C (45°F). A little way south of the Arctic Circle, it has four hours of daylight in December, and 20 hours in June–July.

RIGHT:

Ilulissat, Greenland
A semi-autonomous country under the Danish crown, Greenland is the world's largest island. With around 4,500 inhabitants, Ilulissat is Greenland's third-largest town. Situated on the west coast, 350km (220 miles) north of the Arctic Circle, it makes an excellent vantage point to observe the icebergs and ice floes that break from the ice cap and glaciers, and float into Baffin Bay.

Europe

Europe is a vast peninsula, tapering westwards, with some large offshore islands. Study of its rock types indicates that at one time its north-western part formed a single landmass with northern Canada. Some of its northern coasts are still rising upwards, in a 'bounce-back' effect from being depressed under billions of tonnes of ice in the last Ice Age, which ended about 12,000 years ago. However, the rise in sea level caused by melting of the polar ice is happening faster than this isostatic uplift.

No coast is static. Near Ravenna in eastern Italy, fields stretch over where there was once a Roman naval base. In eastern England, whole settlements have been swallowed up by the sea since the Middle Ages. The force of breaking waves undermines cliffs and carves rocks; coastwise currents shift millions of tonnes of sand and mud. One night's storm can turn a sandy beach into a shingle bank, or back again.

The proximity of large cities has encouraged the development of coastal resorts all round the European coast. For many, it may be enough to lie on a sunny beach or patronize local cafés and bars, but there is always more to do. Coastlands are often bird sanctuaries and protected areas where rare plants may be seen. Even in the more remote and rugged areas, there are likely to be people walking, or engaged in more adventurous activities such as cliff diving, scuba diving, abseiling and 'coasteering', which takes them in and out of the water as they scramble over rocks and explore caves. Certain coastal areas, such as England's Jurassic Coast, are popular with fossil hunters.

OPPOSITE:
Ponta de São Lourenço Madeira, Portugal
Marking the eastern end of Madeira, the Ponta de São Lourenço cape terminates a narrow peninsula of volcanic rock with spectacular cliffs on each side. It is home to many species of seabird as well as the world's rarest seal, the monk seal or seawolf, which can sometimes be seen below the cliffs.

ABOVE:
Fajã do Ouvidor, São Jorge, Azores, Portugal
A fajã is a coastal rock platform formed from fallen cliffs or ancient lava flows: a particular feature of the Azores islands. The Fajã do Ouvidor, with its lava columns, is characterized as a dendritic (branching) type, extending seawards and providing good sites for rod-and-line fishing.

RIGHT:
Ria Formosa, Algarve, Portugal
Close to the fishing town of Olhão, the Ria Formosa Natural Park is a wide area of salt marsh, sand dunes and barrier islands, making up one of the world's most varied and important wetlands. Its coastal forms are constantly shifting under the influence of currents, tides and winds.

OPPOSITE:

Costa Quebrada, Cantabria, Spain

On Spain's north coast between Santander and Valdearenas is the geological phenomenon of the 'broken coast', where tilted rock strata rise from the sea to run parallel with the shoreline, with rock stacks and natural arches. Evidence abounds of ancient coral reefs, tropical forests and fossilized marine ecosystems.

RIGHT:

Denia, Alicante, Spain

The continental edge stretches into the distance from the harbour and resort of Denia. This is Spain's Costa Blanca, rich in sandy coves between rocky headlands, where old fishing villages are now lively tourist resorts, lured both by the beaches, the Mediterranean summers and a rich cultural history.

Flysch Coast, Zumaia, Basque Country, Spain
Flysch is a rock formation in which thin layers of hard sandstone are separated by softer deposits of shale. Over geological time, the layers have been tipped up by the same forces that formed the mountains of northern Spain. The sea has washed away the shale and broken down the sandstone into the rail-like lines at tide-level.

Vulcano, Aeolian Islands, Italy
Smoky and imposing, Gran Cratere looms over the northeastern part of this volcanic island. Named for the Roman god of fire, it has many hot springs, pools and mudbaths. To geologists it is a young island, formed from a series of eruptions around 260,000 years ago. It has been settled by humans since around 4000 BCE.

Grand Canal, Venice, Italy
Nowhere shows the human management of coastline more effectively and beautifully than this. Until around 400 CE, it was no more than tidal mudflats in a great sheltered lagoon. Refugees from the Gothic and Hunnic invasions of Italy began the build-up, which culminated in a magnificent, rich and powerful city. Increasingly prone to flooding, Venice is preparing new defences against storm surges.

PREVIOUS PAGES:
Montenegro, Adriatic Sea
Much of Montenegro's
294-kilometre (183-mile)
coastline is mountainous,
with the Dinaric Alps
plunging straight into the sea.
This view reveals the way that
the salt water has worked its
way into the limestone rock
at the base of the cliffs, while
rainfall permeates through
on the upper surface, forming
caves and tunnels.

ABOVE:
**Ploumanac'h Lighthouse,
Brittany, France**
The rocks on this section
of the Breton coast are
an unusual pink granite,
weathered and eroded into
shapes that often resemble
sleeping seals. The lighthouse
is built of the same stone,
and is reached by a bridge
carrying the 'path of the
revenue-men', on the watch
for smugglers.

RIGHT:
Bonifacio, Corsica, France
On the southern tip of
Corsica, the old citadel
and some of the houses of
Bonifacio find themselves
ever closer to the receding
cliffs. Offshore stacks
show how much has been
eaten away by the sea in
recent centuries. The cliffs
themselves are formed of
sandstone layers, laid down
on an ancient seabed.

**Mont St Michel,
Normandy, France**
Churches dedicated to St
Michael are usually on raised
sites, and this is one of the
most dramatic. Dating back
to the early 8th century CE,
it was gradually enlarged
into a great Benedictine
monastery. Its defensive walls
are testimony to the constant
medieval wars between
France and England. It is still
a monastery today.

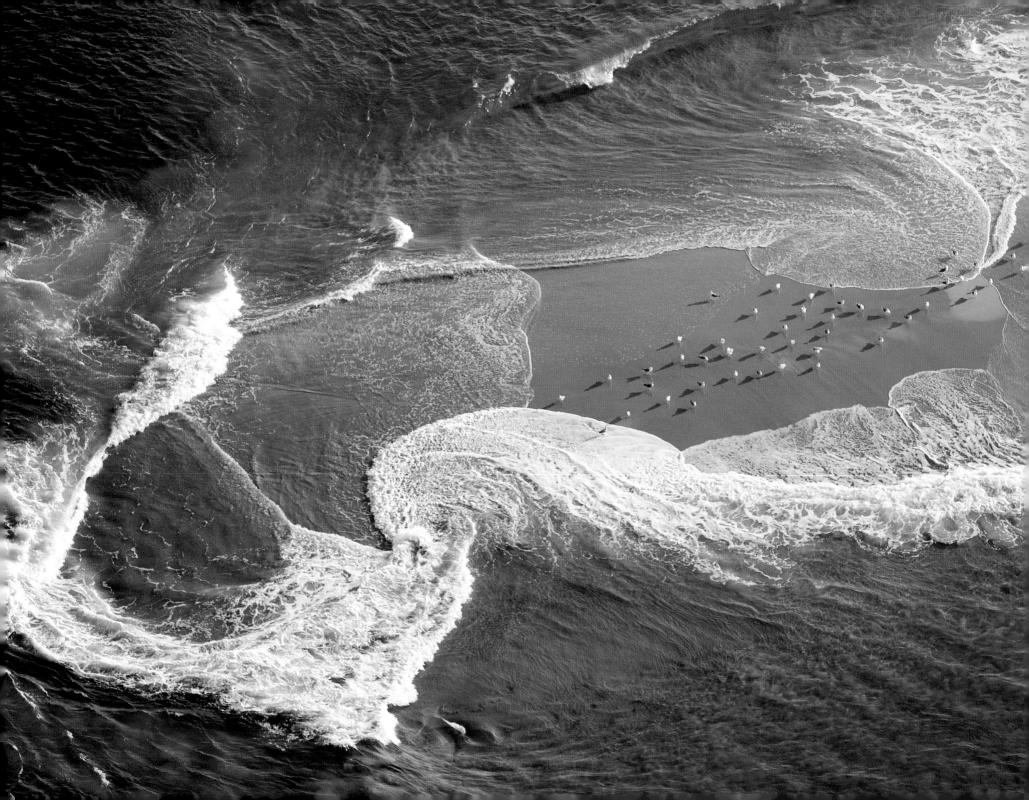

OPPOSITE:

Banc d'Arguin, Bassin d'Arcachon, Gironde, Aquitaine, France
Accessible only by boat, this great sandbank on the Gironde estuary is in constant movement, both in shape and position, due to its location facing the open Atlantic. Its inner side shelters a wide variety of bird-life, both resident and migratory.

RIGHT:

Grand Crohot Beach, Lège-Cap-Ferret, Gironde, Aquitaine, France
A vast sandy beach, open to the Atlantic, with big waves that make it popular with surfers and breezes that attract kite-surfers. There is no town, giving the coastline here a remote and natural air. The sand dunes are planted with special grasses to help maintain stability, and the beach is backed by vast pine forests.

Calanques National Park, Provence, France
'Calanque' is the name given to the steep-sided narrow inlets made by the sea into limestone cliffs on the Provençal coast between Marseille and Cassis. The combination of white cliffs and deep green water is striking. With no topsoil, the rock surface is home to many specialized plant species, and the inaccessibility of cliff nests encourages rare birds.

OPPOSITE:

St Agnes, Cornwall, England
Tin mines have existed in Cornwall since the Bronze Age, with early traders coming from as far as Carthage. Abandoned workings like this one, near the village of St Agnes on the north Cornish coast, are frequent. Only the walls and chimney of the steam-powered engine house remain standing.

RIGHT:

Lizard Point, Cornwall, England
The southernmost point of Great Britain, its name probably derives from the Cornish 'lezou', meaning headland. It is of interest to geologists because of its mix of igneous and metamorphic rocks, including serpentine, a hard, greenish rock with a texture resembling snakeskin, used for decoration in architecture and jewellery.

Ladram Bay, Devon, England

Part of the 'Jurassic Coast', so called because of the rich array of rock formations and fossil remains from the Triassic, Jurassic and Cretaceous periods, Ladram Bay has impressive sea stacks of sandstone. The role played by the sea in exposing the geological and biological history of a landscape formed more than 200 million years ago is particularly clear.

Chesil Beach, Dorset, England

This 28-kilometre (18-mile) bank of pebbles is a tombolo: a sea-created link between two land areas. Dating from the end of the last Ice Age, it has had its present form for around 5,000 years. The lagoon and wetlands on the landward side are designated as an area of Special Scientific Interest.

ABOVE:
Durdle Door, Lulworth Cove, Dorset, England
A natural arch terminating a ridge of hard limestone, Durdle Door probably began as a cave before the sea finally broke right through.

Fossilized remnants of an ancient forest, dating back about 140 million years, can be seen on the upper surface of the 60m (200ft) arch.

RIGHT:
Bat's Head, Devon, England
The once-horizontal layers of chalk have been turned by earth movement to stand vertically. The sea is digging in between the high and low

tide levels and the dark area below the peak shows 'Bat's Hole' where a small sea-worn arch is being enlarged. Wave-driven flint pebbles help to speed up erosion of the chalk.

OPPOSITE:

Blackpool, Lancashire, England

The coast as holiday playground: Blackpool developed in the 19th century as a seaside resort for England's manufacturing cities, with attractions such as music and dance halls, cinemas and amusement arcades to complement its big sandy beach. Like most such resorts, Blackpool has had to reinvent itself to meet contemporary tastes.

LEFT:

Southwold, Suffolk, England

On England's North Sea coast, Southwold is a small, sedate resort, still a fishing harbour, and a haunt of writers and artists. Priding itself on its traditional appearance, it is nevertheless protected by major new works to prevent flooding both from the adjacent river and the gradually rising sea.

OVERLEAF:

Beach Huts, Wells-next-the-Sea, Norfolk, England

Beach huts, owned by families or rented out, are a feature of many resorts on England's eastern coast. They provide shelter and privacy while the family is on the beach. Their great variety of detail and colour within a standard building form makes an attractive backdrop between the beach and the pine forest.

LEFT:

Crosby Beach, Merseyside, England

On the muddy shore just north of Liverpool stands 'Another Place': a group of 100 cast-iron figures of nude males, life-size, gazing seawards. Spread over 3km (1.8 miles) and extending below the tideline, the figures are replicas of the body of its sculptor, Antony Gormley. After temporary installations at Cuxhaven, Germany, Stavanger, Norway, and De Panne, Belgium, they were permanently placed here in 2007.

RIGHT

Bamburgh Castle, Northumberland, England

Bamburgh sums up much of earlier English history. It was the capital of Bernicia, an early kingdom of Anglo-Saxon migrants to Britain. A castle was built here by the Normans in 1086 as a defence against the Scots. It was a strongpoint in the 15th century Wars of the Roses. The present structure is a 19th century 'restoration'.

Bow Fiddle Rock, Moray, Scotland
A rock stack incorporating a natural arch. Formed of metamorphic quartzite (sandstone hardened by immense pressure), tilted by earth movements and buried under newer formations which were later eroded away, Bow Fiddle Rock got its name from the resemblance to the end of a fiddle bow. Just offshore, it was once a test of local bravery to leap onto the rock to gather seagulls' eggs.

Loch Ness, Inverness-shire Scotland
Filling the northeast end of a geological rift extending across the Scottish Highlands, and linked to the sea by canal, Loch Ness holds the largest volume of water of any lake in Great Britain. Its length is 37km (23 miles) and its greatest depth is 240m (788ft). Stories of a monster inhabiting it remain popular, though 'Nessie' is discounted by scientists as a myth.

Giant's Causeway, County Antrim, Northern Ireland
The regular shapes of the 40,000 or so basalt columns and bases, extending into the sea, encouraged the legend of a vast structure built by giants. The truth is hardly less dramatic: some 60 million years ago this was a region of intense volcanic activity and the basalt columns are the result of rapid cooling, with consequent fracturing and contraction into (mostly) hexagonal columns.

OPPOSITE:

Cliffs of Moher, County Clare, Ireland

Bird-haunted, and rising to 214m (702ft) on Ireland's south-west coast, these layered rocks – sandstone, siltstone and shale – were deposited in a vast river system more than 300 million years ago. The wave-line shows where eroded debris lies just below the surface.

RIGHT

Sand-flats near Dundalk, County Louth, Ireland

Relic of a once-intensive inshore fishing industry, an abandoned fishing boat gradually decays on the broad tidal flats of Dundalk Bay. The area is internationally important for waterfowl, with a regular population of more than 20,000 birds, including Brent and Greylag Geese, Great Crested Grebe, Shelduck, Curlew, Dunlin and Wigeon.

Vlissingen, Zeeland, Holland, Netherlands
These poles, placed to stabilize the muddy shoreline, indicate a centuries-long struggle to keep the sea away. Sixty per cent of the Dutch population live below sea level, and the country has a largely artificial coastline, with sea-walls, sluice gates, tidal barriers and emergency flood basins. Satellite observation and other new technologies are creating a 'smart' coastline which senses and responds to storm surges.

LEFT:

Sylt, Schleswig-Holstein, Germany

Sylt is one of the largest Frisian Islands, off the coast of the Netherlands and Germany. Joined to the mainland by a causeway, it is in effect a great sandbank, with its western edge a sandy beach 40km (25 miles) long. Until the 12th century it was part of the mainland, and the shallow, muddy sea separating it is largely uncovered at low tide.

ABOVE:

Fischland, Mecklenburg-Vorpommern, Germany

Germany's Baltic coast is lined by lagoons and sandspits, and Fischland is a narrow neck of land linking the mainland to the Darss peninsula. Once an island, it was converted into a peninsula by the mercantile Hanseatic League in the late 14th century. Its highest point is 18m (60ft) above sea level, and its western side, seen here, is being eroded at a rate of around half a metre a year.

Múlafossur Waterfall, Vágar, Faroe Islands, Denmark

Vágar is the third-largest of the Faroe Islands and this waterfall on its western side is its most famous scenic attraction, spilling 60m (200ft) from the clifftop into the sea. At times of high wind, so much spray is blown upwards as to make it seem that gravity is being reversed.

LEFT:
Near Gothenburg, Sweden
Sweden's western coast has many sheltered bays and inshore islands, rich in shellfish such as the nephrops (Norwegian lobster) and with many opportunities for sea angling for salmon and sea trout. On its exposed site, this hut looks like a fishermen's place for storing and curing fish, though it would certainly provide a good viewing point for seabirds, seals and sea otters.

ABOVE:
Porkkala Peninsula, Finland
In November temperatures on Finland's south coast fall below 0°C (32°F), and the waters of the Gulf of Finland partially freeze over. Evergreen pine trees stand defiantly in a coastal landscape of glaciated and water-worn rocks, covered in snow and decorated with filigree icicles.

OPPOSITE:
Hel Peninsula, Pomerania, Poland
Stretching 35km (22 miles) into the Bay of Gdansk, but only 100m (329ft) wide at its narrowest, this long sandbank is a valued recreational area for the inhabitants of nearby Gdansk. Its strategic location near the country's main port made it a heavily fortified defensive site in World War II, and there is still much evidence to be seen of gun emplacements.

BELOW:
Jurkalne, Latvia
Facing across the Baltic Sea towards the Swedish island of Gotland, this beach looks peaceful but it is part of a fast-eroding coastline. The tree-clad sandy bluffs, up to 20m (70ft) high, which back it, are easily attacked by storm tides and in some years can be pushed back several metres. Stairways down to the beach have to be regularly replaced.

Kaliningrad, Russia
Kaliningrad Province is
a Russian enclave on the
Baltic coast tucked between
Poland and Lithuania. Apart
from the city itself, a string
of small resorts fringes the
sandy beaches, many of
them retaining an old-world
atmosphere.

LEFT:

Segla Peak, Senja Island, Troms, Norway
This striking peak rears 640m (2,100ft) above the Atlantic coast of Norway's second-largest island. Despite its precipitous appearance, Segla can be climbed by energetic walkers, to earn a magnificent 360° view from the summit. Senja is linked to the mainland by the lofty 25-span, 1,147-metre-long (3,763-feet) Gisund Bridge.

RIGHT:

Lofoten, Norway
Despite its remote location, the Lofoten archipelago has good communications, with modern roads, bridges and tunnels traversing the rugged landscape and connecting all the larger islands. Nowhere here is far from the sea and the islands have many hiking trails, both along the shorelines and into the mountains.

Asia

Asia's coastline shows the great variety of landforms and seascapes that are to be expected on the largest continent, where the northern coast meets the Arctic ice and land-masses include the innumerable islands of Indonesia. Such vastness brings extremes, and Asian beaches range from those which are among the world's most beautiful to those which are the world's most despoiled and polluted.

Many coasts in Asia are under threat. Some low-lying island nations, such as the Maldives, face an uncertain future with sea levels predicted to rise by at least 30cm (1ft) by 2050. Bangladesh, with a third of its land surface barely above present sea level, is in a critical situation, made worse by the increasing frequency and violence of tropical storms. The rising sea level is driven by two factors: one is the melting of ice, which is visible and can be measured. The other is the natural propensity of water to expand as it becomes warmer. The oceans have absorbed 90 per cent of the warming of the Earth between 1967 and 2017.

The seas around Asia receive a steady torrent of plastic rubbish, much of which ends up on the tideline. It has been established that around 90 per cent of the plastic discharged into the oceans comes from just ten big rivers, eight of which are in Asia. This is not entirely the fault of the nations through which these rivers flow: vast amounts of plastic rubbish from western countries, formerly sent to China for recycling or disposal, are now shipped to Malaysia and Indonesia.

On a more positive note, Asian countries are working to reduce marine pollution, and they lead on sustainable use of coastland for food production. Eight Asian nations produce 99 per cent of the world's farmed seaweed, about 24 million tonnes a year.

OPPOSITE:
Seaweed farm, Xiapu, Fujian, China
Growing and harvesting kelp has become the mainstay industry of this district on the edge of the East China Sea, with 40sq kilometres (15.4sq miles) of mudflats. The seaweed farms, set in mountain-fringed flatlands, with their wide symmetrical patterns of bamboo stakes, also attract many visitors.

Chaka Saline Lake, Haixi, Qinghai, China
Far from the sea and 3,059m (10,036ft) above it, the shore of this lake is formed of salt crystals and the lake itself is a mixture of liquid and salt. Salt has been extracted here for human use for more than 3,000 years. China has many such lakes but Chaka is considered the most beautiful.

LEFT:

Qingdao, Shandong, China
To the north and south of the bustling port city of Qingdao are forest parks where the wild and rocky shores contrast with the city's beach, which is Asia's largest. Here on China's eastern edge, greenstone and granite rocks form the edge of the North China Craton, a zone where the Earth's crust and mantle have been in relative stability through successive geological eras.

OPPOSITE:

Repulse Bay, Hong Kong
Tall apartment blocks rise above the beach in this residential area of Hong Kong. The beach itself is very clean, but regular trash removal is necessary to get rid of plastic rubbish washed in from the sea, and the water quality is closely monitored.

OPPOSITE:

Rai Leh Beach, Krabi, Thailand

Cut off by limestone bluffs from the main resort, Rai Leh Beach is accessible only by boats, of which there are many. Rai Leh is really a peninsula jutting into the Andaman Sea, with four beaches separated by promontories, but this scenic spot is by far the most-visited.

RIGHT:

Ha Long Bay, Vietnam

More than a thousand islets and isolated rocks are found in this bay. In legend they are jewels showered by a *ha long* (descending dragon) come to protect the people; in reality they are another example of what water does to limestone. These towers and strangely shaped islands have a kind of surreal peace, at variance with Vietnam's war-torn 20th century history.

Near Nha Trang, Vietnam
Rafts, small fishing craft and exposed rocks dot the water in the light of the setting sun near the South Vietnamese resort town of Nha Trang. Just inland there are hot springs, mud-pools, salt fields and magnificent Buddhist temples.

BOTTOM:

Daepo Jusangjeolli, Jeju Island, South Korea
Is this where Northern Ireland's Giant's Causeway ends, or begins? The effects of vulcanism are varied but sometimes the same phenomenon can be found in widely separated places. These hexagonal columns are formed by the cooling and contracting of hot lava flowing up from volcanic vents. It is one of many remarkable natural and cultural sights on Jeju Island.

RIGHT:

Haedong Yonggungsa Temple, Gijang-gun, Busan, South Korea
Begun in 1376 and enlaced with many legends, unusual in its coastal setting, this beautiful Buddhist temple was carefully restored in the 1930s. Its position among rocks and trees, just above the sea, was carefully planned, with all its architectural and decorative details reflecting aspects of Buddhist teaching.

OPPOSITE:

Horseshoe Island, Mergui Archipelago, Myanmar

In the Andaman Sea, close to the border of Myanmar with Thailand, lies this group of small islands, also known as the Myeik Archipelago. Tourism is hardly developed here and most visitors come on boat 'safaris' from the mainland. Despite the unspoiled scenery, much of the local coral has been blighted by dynamite fishing.

RIGHT:

Mannar Island Lighthouse, Talaimannar, Mannar Island, Sri Lanka

In the north of Sri Lanka, Mannar is joined by bridge and causeway to the mainland, but long unvisitable because of civil war. Once a pearl-fishing centre, its history includes occupation by the Portuguese, Dutch and British, who built the lighthouse (now disused) at Talaimannar in 1915.

Gokarna, Karnataka, India
An important place of pilgrimage for Hindus, Gokarna's beaches and beautiful wooded coastline have also made the town a venue for foreign tourists. The area still retains a degree of tradition and simple hospitality, and the many temples give it the distinctive sense of being more than just a tourist town.

LEFT:

Sri Lanka

In Sri Lanka, the prevailing wind comes from the south-west, which may have influenced the growth and angle of this palm tree growing right by the open shore. The island has a wide range of climatic regions, influenced by sea temperatures and currents in coastal areas, but the ruling features are the twice-yearly monsoon rains and intervening dry season.

RIGHT:

Stilt fishing, Sri Lanka

Still practised especially on the southern coasts of Sri Lanka, stilt fishing is not an ancient tradition, but was introduced in the late 1940s at a time of food shortages. Using minimal equipment, it requires effective balance as well as fishing skill. The fishermen catch small inshore fish, spotted herring and mackerel.

Clifton, Karachi, Pakistan
Commonly known as Seaview, this beach has always been popular with Karachi's citizens for sea breezes and bathing, especially during very hot spells. Its urban situation, close to an oil terminal and sewage outfalls, makes pollution a constant hazard. Voluntary groups help to mitigate the problem by clearing rubbish, but official action has been very limited.

Chittagong Shipbreakers, Bangladesh
Along a 29-kilometre (18-mile) stretch of the Bay of Bengal, ships are run ashore to be broken up. The Chittagong shipbreakers are experts at dismantling large vessels but the industry is unregulated and dangerous both for its low-paid workers and for the surrounding environment. Some 90 per cent of the material is recycled but there is scant provision for the removal of toxic waste.

LEFT:

Le Morne, Mauritius
Only visible from above, this phenomenon looks like water pouring downwards below the sea's surface. In fact it is sand washed by currents off the island's coastal shelf and falling into the depths of the Indian Ocean.

ABOVE:

Caspian Sea, near Baku, Azerbaijan
The Caspian is the world's largest inland sea, and its vast basin lies 28m (92ft) below mean sea level. The Abseron Peninsula juts into the middle part of the sea, and the rocks here date back to the formation of the Alps and Caucasus mountains. Large oil deposits in the region have brought prosperity to Azerbaijan's capital, Baku.

OVERLEAF:

Near Aktau, Kazakhstan
Under a stormy sky, the Caspian Sea takes on a threatening aspect. The water in this northern part of the sea is relatively fresh, due to the huge inflow of the Volga River. This view is from its eastern coast, near the new city of Aktau, which was originally a campsite for workers in oil and uranium extraction.

OPPOSITE:

Cape Duana, Aral Sea, Karakalpakstan, Uzbekistan
Diversion of its feeding rivers has caused the drying and desertification of much of the Aral Sea, a huge ecological disaster to what had been until the 1960s the world's fourth-largest inland sea. In this remote region, below the Ustyurt Plateau, the sea's deepest part survives, though even here the water has receded a kilometre from the former shoreline.

LEFT:

Batumi, Adjara, Georgia
Like an abstract painting, four bands of colour and texture make up this sunset image from the Black Sea's eastern coast.
Batumi is Georgia's second-largest city, and its beach of multicoloured pebbles, in contrast to the empty scene here, is normally crowded.

OPPOSITE:
Kobuleti, Adjara, Georgia
The long beach in this Black Sea resort is formed of coarse dark sand and pebbles. Kobuleti is a good place to experience Georgia's mix of European and Asian traditions and cultures, making it popular with visitors from Turkey and Armenia, though relations with Russia have been tense since it gained independence from the former Soviet Union in 1991.

RIGHT
Rubini Rock, Hooker Island, Franz Josef Land, Arkhangelsk Oblast, Russia
A close-up of the 'organ pipe' structure of this massive volcanic rock at the north-western edge of Hooker Island. The opportunities for exploring geomorphology and pursuing climate study and biological diversity make this an area of special interest to scientists. Apart from a huge seabird colony, walrus, bowhead whales and polar bears can all be seen.

ABOVE:

Ust-Barguzin, Lake Baikal, Russia
These blue waves ripple over the world's deepest lake, more than 1,600m (5,250ft) deep. In terms of volume, Lake Baikal is also the largest of all freshwater lakes. Far longer than it is wide, it fills a massive rift caused by earth movements more than 25 million years ago. It is not wholly landlocked, with one river flowing outwards to the Yenisei and the Kara Sea.

RIGHT:

Lake Baikal, Russia
The immense age and isolation of Lake Baikal have led to the development of many unique species, including the golomyanka fish, which gives birth to live young. The lake supports a single mammal species, the Baikal seal. Plant life is also rich and varied at surface level and round the margins, and the area is home to some 320 bird species.

Lake Baikal, Russia
The extent of Lake Baikal helps to give its surroundings a milder climate than the Siberian average. Even so, it normally freezes over between January and May, enabling such activities as skating, ice-biking, snowmobiling and ice-fishing. In summer the water is warm enough to swim in: local lore says that a dip in Baikal adds five years to one's life.

Biya River, Lake Teletskoye, Altai Republic, Russia
Trees fringe this deep lake (325m; 1,066ft) in a glaciated valley. On all sides the banks are steep but there are some beach areas. Its name means 'Golden Lake', alluding to the legend of a man who found a gold ingot that was useless for any of his normal purposes. So he threw it in the lake.

Tobizin Cape, Russkiy Island, near Vladivostok, Russia
Stretching seawards, this rocky headland is a striking feature of Russia's Pacific coast. Exposed rock formations from the Triassic era once formed an ocean floor: now their rounded, weathered surfaces impress visitors. There are remnants of World War II defences, and an iron lighthouse, rusty and disused, stands at the tip.

LEFT:

Kamchatka Peninsula, Russia

In Russia's far north-east, Kamchatka is a wild and rugged landscape with much live volcanic activity, making it a land of ice and fire in winter. This view, on the eastern coast, looks over cliffs of tuff (hardened volcanic ash). Thinly populated by people, the peninsula has one of the world's highest populations of brown bears.

OPPOSITE:

Vilyuchinski volcano, Kamchatka, Russia

Rising behind the cliffs and rock stacks of Avacha Bay on Kamchatka's south-eastern coast, the extinct volcano of Vilyuchinski rises to 2,175m (7,136ft). Twenty-nine volcanoes in the region are still active. On this huge bay also lie the regional capital, Petropavlovsk-Kamchatky, and Russia's Pacific Fleet submarine base at Vilychik.

Africa
& The Middle East

The African continent presents a much smoother and more regular outline than the others, the result of uplifting of most of the land-mass during the past 180 million years. The present coastal plains, often lying below steep escarpment slopes, were once part of the undersea continental shelf. One consequence of this is that Africa has relatively few natural harbours, which require bays and deep inlets. Despite being the second-largest continent, after Asia, Africa's coastline is shorter than that of Europe, the smallest continent, which is far more indented and penetrated by the sea.

Historically, African nations have been more concerned with the resources of their inland areas than with the economic development of coastal areas. This view is gradually changing, as concern grows for the condition of the world's oceans and their fundamental importance to climate stability, to food supply and to international trade. Development and sustainable use of coastal areas is very much part of this. The so-called Blue Economy is concerned with the exploitation and preservation of the marine environment into the future so that it continues and expands as a major resource. Kenya and the Seychelles are among the countries driving this forward.

The Middle East embraces the deeps of the Red Sea and Persian Gulf, and also holds the world's lowest-lying coastline, round the saline waters of the Dead Sea, far below mean sea level.

OPPOSITE:
Legzira Beach, Tiznit, Morocco
A stark reminder of the fragility of coastal scenery: this massive arch, formed of red sandstone resting on a base of granite and for long a feature of Legzira and an attraction for visitors, collapsed abruptly in September 2016, cutting the beach in two. Its neighbour, seen through the now-vanished arch, still survives.

Rabat, Morocco
Below the wall of the Medina in Rabat fishing boats are moored in the estuary of the Bou Regreg River. Of traditional design and colour, their sterns are cut to allow for the fixing of outboard motors. Although the anchorage is sheltered, it can be tricky to enter and leave when a strong northwesterly swell is coming from the Atlantic.

OPPOSITE:

Bay of Tangier, Morocco
For Europeans, Tangier, the nearest African city to their continent, has always been a place of exoticism and mystery. Writers and artists came here to celebrate liberation from the restrictive attitudes of their own cultures. Phoenicians, Berbers, Romans, Arabs and, later, Spanish and French have all contributed to the ambiance of this multicultural city.

RIGHT:

Oran, Algeria
Oran, with one of the few big natural harbours on Africa's Mediterranean coast, was the site of a highly controversial episode in July 1940, when, after the fall of France, a British squadron bombarded ships of the French Mediterranean Fleet moored here at the naval base of Mers-el-Kebir, to prevent them from falling under Axis control.

Nile River, Aswan, Egypt
Looking upstream over the Nile River's sandy shoreline, with Aswan City in the distance. Satellites measure the water level, closely monitored by the 11 Nile Basin countries.
Sailing feluccas offer cruises on this historic stretch of the 6,650-kilometre (4,130-mile) long river.

Blue Hole Diving Site, Sinai, Egypt
Marked out by its deeper blue than the surrounding water, this 100m (330ft) deep sinkhole has become a magnet for daring or experienced scuba divers. It is 80m (262ft) wide and at a depth of 56m (184ft) there is an exit into the open waters of the Red Sea. Ignoring safety precautions, many divers have died in the Blue Hole.

LEFT:

Beached Ship, Somalia
Piracy on the Somali coast
began with fishermen
protecting their grounds
against foreign vessels
and escalated into attacks
on merchant shipping.
International action had
quelled this activity by
2018, but this factory ship,
abandoned because of
a refusal to pay ransom,
remains as evidence of the
deadly period.

ABOVE:

**Nabuyatom Crater,
Lake Turkana, Kenya**
At the southern end of Lake
Turkana stands this almost
perfectly round caldera,
the remnant of a collapsed
volcano. The lake is the
world's largest in a desert
zone, and also the largest
body of alkaline water. Some
of the earliest evidence of
human ancestor species has
been found in its vicinity.

Lamu Archipelago, Kenya

Two degrees south of the
Equator, near the Kenya-
Somali border, these islands
are intrinsically peaceful
places, where transport is
likely to be by donkey or
sailing dhow, and where the
preservation of traditional
Swahili culture provides a
special insight into the life of
pre-colonial Africa.

**Pangane, Cabo Delgado,
Mozambique**

An archetypal tropical beach
scene – Pangane has been
described by visitors as a
tranquil and beautiful place,
where locals go to sea in their
outrigger boats to catch fish
that are cooked and eaten on
the same day.

LEFT:

Anse Source d'Argent Beach, La Digue, Seychelles

The silvery name is appropriate to this beach of white sand on the Seychelles' third-largest island, named after an 18th-century French exploration vessel. Wildlife here includes the paradise flycatcher (in danger of extinction), giant tortoises and coconut crabs. Its massive granite rocks are remnants of the ancient supercontinent known as Gondwana.

OPPOSITE:

Hawsbill Turtles, Cousine Island, Seychelles

One of the most remarkable sights of the natural world is the emergence of baby turtles from their eggs laid in the sand and making their way unerringly down to the sea. These hawksbill turtles (*Eretmochelys imbricata*) are one of two species that nest in the Seychelles. Increasingly rare, hawksbill turtles are now classified as critically endangered.

Inhassorro, Inhambane, Mozambique
Fishermen prepare their craft for night fishing at this small port. The Bay of Inhassorro has reefs which harbour many species of fish, including manta and eagle rays, and moray eels, as well as dolphins, turtles and dugongs. Offshore are the Bazaruto Islands, a national underwater park.

Mossel Bay, Western Cape, South Africa
Breaking waves show why this is a prime surfing location. People have been here a very long time: the Mossel Bay Archaeology Project was established to explore caves on this coastline which may have harboured Middle Stone Age communities. These were possibly the earliest humans to use dyes and develop specialized stone tools.

Cape Town, South Africa
These massive interlocking concrete blocks are known as *dolosse* (singular *dolos*) and weigh up to 80 tonnes (79 tons). A South African invention in the 1960s, they are intended to absorb and dissipate the energy of the waves, and are backed by quarried hard rock to form a solid revetment against sea erosion. Dolosse are now used on vulnerable coastlines across the world.

Skeleton Coast, Namibia
Along the 500-kilometre (311-mile) stretch of Namibia's coast, land and sea meet in surprising ways. Lions, cheetahs and hyenas may be seen searching for seals along the sand (Cape fur seals breed here in large numbers). The coast's grim name comes partly from the scattered bones of animals, partly from many shipwrecks, and also from its barren appearance.

Volta River, Ghana
Most of Ghana forms the basin of the Volta River, though the river itself rises further inland, in Burkina Faso. In all, the river is 1,600km (1,000 miles) long. As it widens, the Volta is spanned by the 336m (1,102ft) Adomi Bridge (pictured).

Lobé Falls, Kribi, Cameroon
In the rainy season, water
flowing from the jungle
cascades across a broad front
at Lobé Falls directly into
the Atlantic. The highest
fall is 20m (66ft). For local
inhabitants the falls are a
sacred place, and one of the
tasks of conservators of the
site is to maintain a balance
between its increasing
popularity as a tourist
spectacle, and its historic and
spiritual significance.

Dead Sea, Israel
The lowest area on dry land
in the world, the Dead Sea
basin is 430m (1,410ft) below
mean sea level. Fed by the
River Jordan, it has no outlet.
Its intensely saline water, and
the surrounding black mud,
rich in salts and minerals, is
used for therapies. The sea's
level has fallen by around 30m
(100ft) since the mid-20th
century, due to diversion of
water from the River Jordan.

Dead Sea, Jordan
Heavy evaporation often creates a misty effect over the Dead Sea. As its name suggests, it contains no animal life other than bacteria. Salt-tolerating plants grow in patches along the shoreline, but the basin is largely barren and desolate.

PREVIOUS PAGE
Assad Reservoir, Euphrates Valley, Ar Raqqah, Syria
The largest lake in Syria was formed in 1974 behind the Tabqa Dam on the Euphrates river. The extreme aridity of the surrounding countryside is apparent. The reservoir provides Aleppo's water supply and irrigation to farms, as well as a hydro-electric plant, but has never reached its projected level of supply.

LEFT:

Mediterranean Coast, Turkey
Almost 1,600km (990 miles) long, the aptly named 'Turquoise Coast' of Turkey's Mediterranean region is a magnificent sweep of hills, cliffs and sheltered bays, with the Taurus Mountains behind. Greco-Roman and prehistoric sites, from entire ruined cities to isolated tombs, are to be found in many places.

OPPOSITE:

Narlikuyu, Mersin, Turkey
At Narlikuyu on Turkey's Mediterranean coast, three layers of rock display geological history. The metamorphic bedrock is resistant to sea erosion, while the sedimentary layer resting on it has been pushed further back. More recent deposits of shells and gravels on the top are tipped over when the cliff collapses.

Mediterranean Coast, Turkey
The thinly populated
mountainous hinterland of
the Turquoise Coast has been
traversed by many armies,
from ancient Hittites and
Assyrians to Roman legions,
medieval crusaders and the
conquering Turks. The Holy
Roman Emperor Frederick
Barbarossa was drowned in
the Saleph River in 1190, as
his crusader army came down
from the mountains towards
the sea.

LEFT:

Salt Lake, Iran
After the Caspian Sea, Lake Urmia was the second-largest saltwater lake in the Middle East, but it has shrunk by almost 80 per cent in the past 30 years because of the diversion of its rivers for irrigation, reduced rainfall and greater evaporation caused by hotter air temperatures. Most of the lake bed is now a vast expanse of salt flats.

RIGHT

Musandam, Oman
Strategically placed on the Strait of Hormuz, the entry into the Persian Gulf, the Musandam Governorate is separated from the rest of Oman by the United Arab Emirates. These sharp crags look like a glaciated landscape but the mountains are caused by tectonic action, with the Arabian plate gradually pushing under the Eurasian plate, creating a fjord-like coastscape.

Al-Jalali Fort, Bandar al Khayran, Muscat, Oman
Fortifications guarded the harbour entrance here even before Portuguese occupiers built this fort on the eastern approach, and another on the west, in the 1580s. From the late Middle Ages, Muscat was an important trading centre for spices, timber and silk, and the Portuguese conquest in 1507 was intended to confirm their control of the maritime route.

Qalansiya Beach, Detwah Lagoon, Socotra Island, Yemen
Socotra is a tropical island of magnificent beaches, with many endemic animal and plant species. Its Sanskrit name means 'paradise', but it has suffered from the conflict in Yemen and has to some extent been taken over by the neighbouring United Arab Emirates.

Qalansiya Beach, Socotra Island, Yemen
Socotra's unique plants include the desert rose and the cucumber tree. Specialized bird species include the Jouanin's Petrel, which breeds on the island's cliffs.

The Pacific, Atlantic & Antarctica

The Pacific, Indian and South Atlantic Oceans encircle the Earth in a continuous belt of open sea, bordered by the coastline of Antarctica, the tips of South America and Africa, and the south coasts of Australia and New Zealand's South Island. This chapter reaches as far up as Japan, in the Western Pacific, includes the equatorial islands of Indonesia, tropical and sub-tropical Australia, and stretches down to the frigid, ice-covered continent of Antarctica. Such a wide geographical range offers a huge variety of coastal features and formations, from those heavily modified by human action to those entirely shaped by natural forces. The influence of climate does not go deep, but the heat of the interior can make itself felt even through an ice cap. Geoscientists have found much evidence of vulcanism below western Antarctica, with volcanic heat making the Pine Island Glacier, flowing into the Amundsen Sea, the fastest-melting in the entire continent.

Antarctica's true coastline is largely invisible. Only on some five per cent of the coast is the actual land surface exposed. The rest consists of ice-covered land reaching to the sea, or of massive ice shelves extending far beyond the land and floating on the sea. These are extensions of glaciers: the freshwater ice which forms them continues to move outwards, eventually breaking off as giant icebergs. In addition, in the winter season the extent of sea ice, formed from salt water, greatly extends the frozen zone.

OPPOSITE:
Miho No Matsubara Beach, Shizuoka, Japan
Associated with Japanese legends, the beach at Miho No Matsubara also gives a fine view of sacred Mount Fuji, a dormant volcano 3,776m (12,388ft) high. Its last eruption was in 1707, when its conical form took shape, and the profile of the beach dates from then.

Kushimoto, Wakayama, Japan
The rocks at the southernmost tip of Japan's main island, Honshu, are said to be the remains of a bridge planned by the 8th–9th century Buddhist priest and poet Kobo Daishi, but thwarted by a demon.

Hatago Iwa Rock, Noto Peninsula, Ishikawa, Japan
On the eastern shore of the Sea of Japan, these rocks are considered a sacred place in the Shinto cult, and many legends have grown up about them. The linking rope between the small shrines on each rock, known as a *shimenawa*, indicates a holy place.

OPPOSITE:
Hualien, Taiwan
Hualien's name refers to 'eddying waters' at the base of the grand mountain slopes that form the central part of Taiwan's eastern coastline. A spectacular road twists and tunnels along a man-made ledge. The slope continues under the water, to a depth of around 4,000m (13,120ft).

RIGHT:
Near Hatta Island, Maluku, Indonesia
Remote and (so far) free of modern development, the Banda Islands are said to be the original source of nutmeg. Hatta is an island with a few beach villages, reliant on rainfall for its water supply, and surrounded by coral reefs rich in tropical fish from the tiniest up to hammerhead sharks.

Padar Island, Komodo National Park, Indonesia
The beaches on each side of Padar's rocky spine have different coloured sand, white and black, sedimentary and volcanic respectively. Another is pink, of red coral mixed with white sand. No longer inhabited by komodo dragons, the island is still surrounded by a great variety of aquatic life.

Sanur Beach, Bali, Indonesia
In typical Balinese style the sea walls at this southeastern beach are provided with temple structures housing protective statues. Other traditional features can be seen in the design of the houses and of the fishing boats drawn up on the beach.

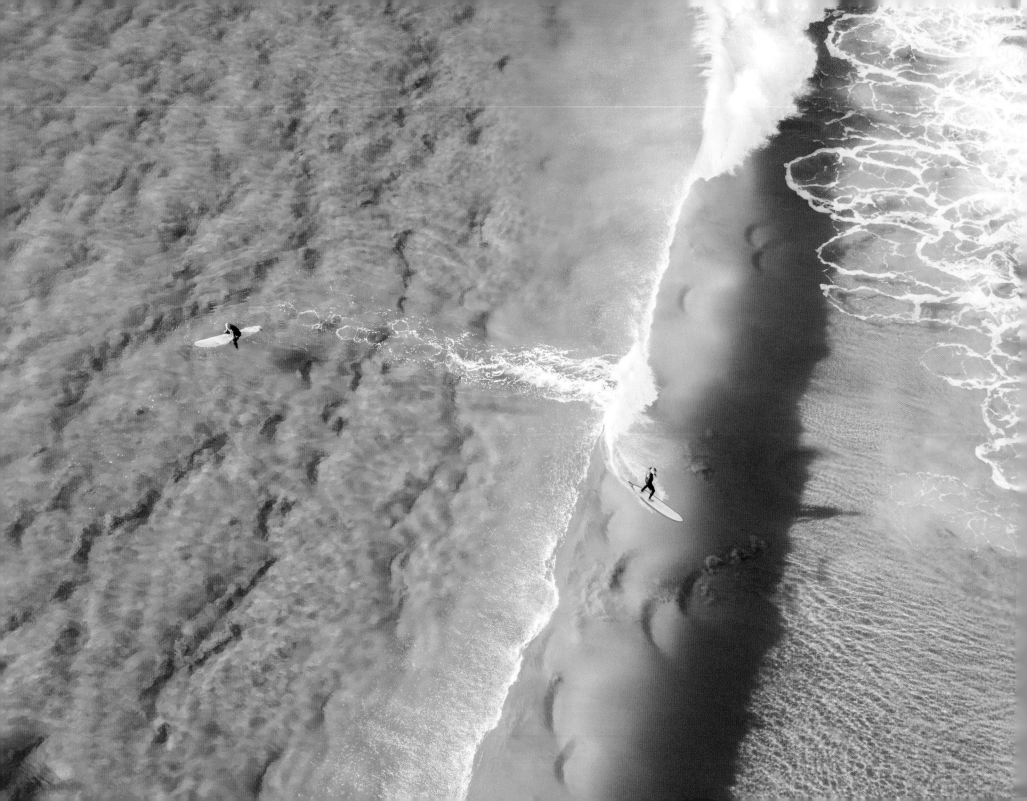

OPPOSITE:

Gold Coast, Queensland, Australia

Pacific waves that have travelled thousands of miles eventually break on the low-lying southern coast of Queensland, building up a shoreline of sandbanks, shallow creeks and long stretches of golden beach. It's no surprise that one of the communities on this coast should have taken the name of Surfers Paradise, once the name of a single hotel, in 1925.

RIGHT:

Surfers Paradise, Gold Coast City, Queensland, Australia

Since 1958 the string of coastal settlements south of Brisbane have grown into a linear city, with the skyscrapers of Surfers Paradise marking its commercial and entertainment centre. Though some areas of rainforest lie inland, this is a coast entirely dominated by human development.

Great Barrier Reef, Queensland, Australia
A segment of the 2,600-kilometre (1,625-mile) coral ecosystem which has been described as the largest living thing on Earth. More than 600 varieties of coral are found on the Great Barrier Reef and it is host to an incalculable number of marine species, both animal and plant. Its future as a living entity is a source of serious concern due to ocean warming and increasing acidification.

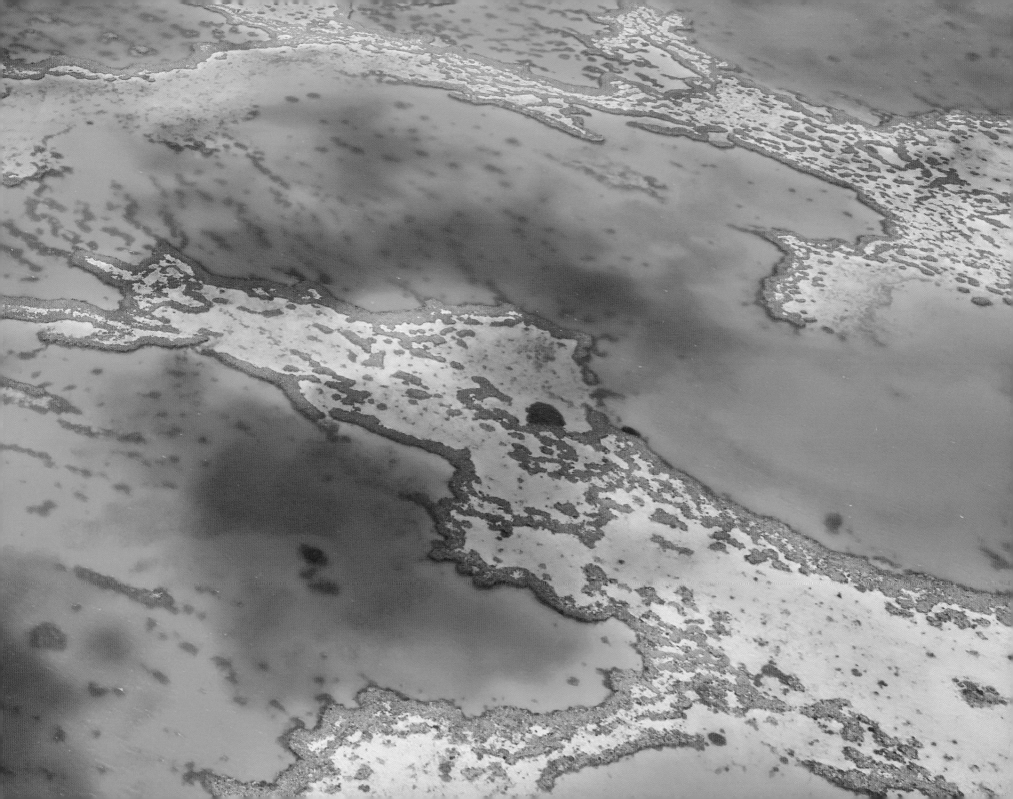

Near Narooma, New South Wales, Australia

Curving breakwaters mark the entry into the Wagonga Inlet, once a broad river valley and now both a holiday playground area and a location of oyster farms. The resort town of Narooma, alongside, is a centre for land and sea-based activities.

Noosa National Park, Sunshine Coast, Queensland, Australia

North of Brisbane is Queensland's Sunshine Coast, with Noosa National Park on a stretch of unspoiled rocky shore. The rock here is sandstone which was subjected to heat or pressure deep underground, and when exposed, gradually weathers and breaks up along the joints and cracks.

Antarctic Sound
Named in 1902 for Carl Anton Larsen's Swedish exploration ship *Antarctic*, this birthplace of giant icebergs lies between the northern end of the Antarctic Peninsula and Joinville Island. The bergs break away from the Larsen Ice Shelf and float out into the open ocean.

Koekohe Beach, Otago, South Island, New Zealand
Like immense stone footballs, these boulders lie on the beach at Moeraki. They are formed from layers of calcite which accumulated around the fragmentary remains of plants and shellfish, and date back some 60 million years.

Mount Maunganui,
Bay of Plenty, North Island, New Zealand
A coastal path on Mount Maunganui. A sense of flow still
remains in the exposed rhyolite lava of this extinct volcanic
cone which stands at the entrance to Tauranga Harbour.
Rhyolite is highly viscous, fine-grained and slow flowing.

ABOVE:
Punakaiki, South Island, New Zealand
Water action has sculpted the coastal limestone into all
sorts of strange formations, often resembling stacked pan-
cakes. Sea-bored tunnels lead to blowholes which spout
when waves surge in.

OPPOSITE:
Mitre Peak, Milford Sound, South Island, New Zealand
Rising 1,692m (5,560ft) above the sea, this mountain, Rahotu in Maori, offers more than a mile of precipitous bare rock. First climbed in 1911, it now has six identified routes to the summit.

LEFT:
Muriwai Beach, North Island, New Zealand
On the west coast of the Auckland region, the rocks above the beach of black volcanic sand are home to a long-established colony of gannets, some 1200 pairs, which nest and breed here between August and March. The Australasian gannet has a wingspan of up to 1.8m (6ft).

LEFT:
Orongo, Easter Island
Here was the centre of the birdman cult on Easter Island. From this clifftop site bird hunters went down and swam out to the islet of Moto Nui (pictured at the top of the photograph). The first to bring back a seabird's egg of the new nesting season achieved high status for himself and his sponsor.

ABOVE:
The Neck, Saunders Island, Falkland Islands
The fourth-largest of the Falkland Island group (also known as the Malvinas Islands), Saunders is a vast sheep farm, home also to many bird species, including the black-browed albatross, rockhopper penguins, steamer ducks, and the striated caracara, known locally as the Johnny rook.

OPPOSITE:

Astrolabe Needle, Brabant Island, British Antarctic Territory

First discovered by a French expedition in 1903, and named for Dumont d'Urville's 19th century exploration vessel *L'Astrolabe*, this monolith rises 50m (164ft) from the sea.

RIGHT:

Andersson Island, Antarctic Sound

A rocky archipelago lies at the tip of the Antarctic Peninsula, far enough north to lose snow cover in the summer months. First named Rosamel after a French admiral in 1838, this islet was renamed Ile de l'Uruguay in 1902 and acquired its present name in honour of a Swedish geologist in 1949.

OVERLEAF:

St Andrews Bay, South Georgia

Elephant and fur seals, king penguins and huge colonies of other seabirds now share this beach with transient human visitors in the cruising season. Claimed for Great Britain by Captain Cook in 1775, the island was used by sealers and whalers until 1964.

Picture Credits